TRUFFLE CULTIVATION

ALL THE SECRETS AND TECHNIQUES OF TRUFFLE GROWING

KARL BROWN

Foreword

Truffle growing, for many, represents a fertile ground where tradition, innovation and passion intertwine in a harmonious symphony. It is not just an agricultural activity, but an exciting journey that has its roots in the millenary bond between man and nature. This book was born from the desire to make the fascination and challenges of this unique practice accessible to everyone, offering a complete and detailed guide for anyone wishing to approach this extraordinary world.

In recent decades, truffle cultivation has gone from being a rarity to a concrete possibility for farmers and enthusiasts. Thanks to scientific advances in mycorrhization, improved soil management techniques and access to new knowledge, it is now possible to successfully grow one of the world's finest products. Yet, despite these innovations, truffle cultivation retains its aura of mystery intact, requiring dedication, study and respect for the rhythms of nature.

On these pages, you will find not only technical information, but also stories, experiences and practical advice, the result of the contribution of expert truffle growers and professionals in the sector. Each chapter is designed to accompany you step by step, from the first approaches to the choice of soil and mycorrhizal plants, up to the strategies for collecting, preserving and enhancing the truffle. Particular attention was paid to contemporary challenges, such as climate change, sustainability and the use of innovative technologies to monitor and improve production.

This book is aimed at everyone: farmers who want to diversify their business, entrepreneurs who see truffle cultivation as a new economic opportunity, and enthusiasts who dream of cultivating a small piece of land and harvesting their own truffles. It is, above all, an invitation to rediscover the value of patience, care and attention to detail, fundamental elements for those who decide to embark on this adventure.

Whether you are a beginner or an expert, our goal is to inspire, inform and guide you on your journey, so that you can make the most of this experience and contribute, in your own way, to preserving and spreading the culture of truffles.

With gratitude for the wonderful natural world that such a treasure gives us, we wish you a good journey into truffle growing.

About the Author

SUMMARY

Chapter 1: History and culture of the truffle

- Historical origin of the truffle
- The truffle in mythology and literature
- Evolution of truffle consumption and hunting
- Truffle growing: from spontaneous activity to structured agricultural practice

Chapter 2: Types of truffles and their characteristics

- Classification of truffles: white, black, summer, winter
- Description of the main species: Tuber magnatum, Tuber melanosporum, Tuber aestivum, Tuber brumale
- Organoleptic and market differences
- Natural habitats of each species

Chapter 3: Truffle Biology

- Truffle life cycle
- Symbiotic interaction with host plants

- Ideal soils and microclimates
- Factors Affecting Production

Chapter 4: Soil Preparation

- Location selection and soil analysis
- pH correction and substrate preparation
- Choice of mycorrhizal plants
- Implantation techniques

Chapter 5: Choosing Host Plants

- Most suitable trees: downy oak, holm oak, hazelnut, hornbeam
- Compatibility of plants with different truffle species
- Mycorrhization: techniques and certifications

Chapter 6: Management of the truffle ground

- Irrigation and water management
- Pruning and plant care
- Weed Control
- Soil Health Monitoring

Chapter 7: Diseases and Pests

- Main threats to truffle production

- Prevention and control methods
- Biological and chemical treatments

Chapter 8: Truffle Harvesting

- Research and collection techniques
- Use of truffle dogs: training and care
- Collection regulations
- Truffle storage after harvesting

Chapter 9: Economic and Trade Aspects

- Truffle market: supply, demand and prices
- How to start a truffle growing business
- Certifications and direct sales
- Export opportunities

Chapter 10: Innovations in truffle cultivation

- New mycorrhization techniques
- Use of technology to monitor truffle fields
- Sustainability and organic farming

Chapter 11: Truffle Cooking

- Gastronomic history of truffles
- Traditional and modern recipes

- Pairings with wines and other dishes
- Truffle storage and processing

Chapter 12: Experiences and Testimonies

- Tales of expert truffle growers
- Successes and difficulties in starting a truffle farm
- Practical tips for newbies

Chapter 1: History and culture of the truffle

Historical origin of the truffle

The truffle, known since ancient times, has been venerated and consumed in different historical eras, taking on different cultural and symbolic roles. Its historical origin is intertwined with myths, legends and culinary discoveries that have fueled its fascination to the present day.

Prehistory and early traces

The origins of truffle consumption probably date back to prehistoric times, when primitive man, driven by necessity, explored the underground to collect roots and mushrooms. Truffles, discovered accidentally, were used as food for their nutritional contribution and their abundance in wooded areas.

Classical antiquity

Egypt: The Egyptians were among the first to consider truffles a special food. Although not many written records have survived, it is known that they were eaten cooked in ashes and accompanied by spices and other seasonings. For this civilization, the truffle represented a gift from the gods, a mysterious creation linked to the elements of nature.

Ancient Greece: Greek philosophers and physicians became interested in truffles, not only as a food, but also as an object of study. Plutarch suggested that the truffle was formed by the union of water, lightning and terrestrial heat. For the ancient Greeks, it was also a symbolic food, often associated with vital energy and aphrodisiac properties.

Ancient Rome: The Romans perfected the use of truffles in the kitchen, elevating it to a symbol of luxury and refinement. Pliny the Elder, in his *Naturalis Historia*, described truffles as "miracles of nature." The truffle was present at the banquets of the patricians and at imperial dinners, where it was served with elaborate culinary preparations. Apicius, a famous Roman gastronome, included truffles in many recipes in his treatise on cooking. For the Romans, the truffle represented the pinnacle of gastronomic and cultural pleasure.

Middle Ages

With the advent of the Middle Ages, the truffle temporarily fell into oblivion. During this time, its underground origin and irregular appearance aroused suspicion. In some cultures, it was considered an obscure food, sometimes associated with evil or esoteric practices. However, truffles continued to be harvested in some rural regions, where they were consumed as a poor food or used in simple preparations.

Renaissance

In the Renaissance, the truffle experienced a cultural and gastronomic renaissance. Thanks to the revaluation of nature and gastronomy as art forms, the truffle once again became the protagonist on the tables of European courts. In

Italy, it was particularly appreciated in the courts of the Medici and Gonzaga, where it was considered a noble ingredient.

In France, Catherine de' Medici introduced the use of truffles in court cuisine, making it popular among the aristocracy. During this period, the truffle began to be studied more systematically, and the belief that it could be cultivated in a controlled manner took hold, an idea that would only be applied in the following centuries.

Modern age and birth of truffle cultivation

In the eighteenth century, the dwindling of natural truffle reserves and the growing demand prompted the search for methods to cultivate truffles. In France, Joseph Talon and Auguste Rousseau were among the first to demonstrate that truffles could be cultivated by planting mycorrhizal trees. These experiments marked the beginning of modern truffle cultivation, opening up new possibilities for production and marketing.

Contemporary era

Today, the truffle is a symbol of luxury and elite gastronomy. Its history, from prehistoric times to the present day, has transformed it from a mysterious delight of nature to a controlled product grown with advanced techniques. Its storied origins, steeped in legend and fascination, continue to inspire chefs, researchers, and enthusiasts around the world.

Evolution of truffle consumption and hunting

Man's relationship with the truffle has gone through centuries of evolution, changing profoundly according to the historical, cultural and social context. From a spontaneously harvested food to a symbol of luxury and sophistication, the consumption and search for truffles has undergone a significant transformation, thanks to the advancement of knowledge and the growing demand.

Antiquity: the truffle as a mysterious and precious food

Already in ancient civilizations, the truffle was prized for its unique flavor and rarity. However, its underground origin made it shrouded in mystery.

In Greece, truffles were considered a precious food, and their presence at banquets indicated wealth and culture. They were often associated with magical or divine properties, fueling interest in their origin.

In Rome, truffle hunting began to be more systematic. Truffles were harvested in specific natural areas, often known for their abundance, and served in elaborate recipes. Their rarity made them a food reserved for the upper classes.

Middle Ages: suspicion and limited use

During the Middle Ages, the consumption of truffles declined due to the cultural climate of the time. The Church, suspicious of everything that could not be easily explained, looked with distrust at the truffle for its hidden origin. It was associated with magic, the devil or esoteric practices. However, in some rural areas, truffles continued to be harvested and consumed. The research was limited to individuals who knew the places where they grew spontaneously, often passing on harvesting techniques orally.

Renaissance: the rebirth of the truffle

With the Renaissance, the perception of the truffle changed radically. It was once again appreciated for its gastronomic qualities and its connection with nature.

European courts: In this period, the truffle became the protagonist in the kitchens of the Italian and French courts. Its rarity made it an exclusive food, a symbol of refinement and power.

The search for truffles became more structured: experienced hunters (often accompanied by pigs or dogs not specifically trained) explored the woods to find these precious mushrooms.

Modern age: the truffle as a commercial product

- In the eighteenth and nineteenth centuries, the growing demand for truffles in European markets led to an increasingly organized search.

- **France**: Truffle hunting became an important economic activity. Trained dogs began to be used, since pigs, although effective in searching, tended to eat truffles once found.

Italy: Regions such as Piedmont, Umbria and Marche became famous for the spontaneous production of truffles. The harvest was mainly concentrated in wooded areas, where experts knew the ideal soil and seasons.

The availability of wild truffles, however, began to decline due to logging and agricultural intensification. This stimulated the development of truffle cultivation, which began to take its first steps with cultivation experiments on mycorrhizal trees.

Contemporary era: from gastronomic excellence to science

Today, the consumption and search for truffles are highly specialized and closely linked to the luxury gastronomic market.

Organized Search: Spontaneous harvesting has evolved into a professional activity, with truffle hunters using dogs trained specifically to spot truffles underground. This practice is regulated by regulations, which protect the environment and biodiversity.

Truffle growing: Thanks to decades of scientific research, it is possible to cultivate truffles through symbiosis with specific trees (oak, hazelnut, hornbeam). This technique has made it possible to increase the availability of the product, while maintaining high quality standards.

Modern consumption

In the twenty-first century, the truffle has become a global symbol of gastronomic excellence. Internationally renowned chefs use it in innovative dishes, enhancing its unique aroma. The truffle industry has expanded, including not only the fresh product, but also oils, creams and other derivatives.

Today, the search for and consumption of truffles represent a synthesis of tradition, innovation and culture, making it one of the most iconic and desired foods in the world.

Truffle growing: from spontaneous activity to structured agricultural practice

Truffle cultivation is the agricultural practice that allows truffles to be cultivated through the symbiotic association between fungi and tree or shrub plants. It is an activity that has undergone a significant evolution, passing from a spontaneous harvest, linked exclusively to nature and local traditions, to a scientific and structured system based on advanced knowledge of mycology, ecology and agronomy.

Origins of truffle growing: from the first observations to cultivation

Until the eighteenth century, truffles were harvested exclusively in the wild. Natural wooded areas were the main sources of truffles, and harvesting was a seasonal activity conducted by expert gatherers, often aided by pigs or dogs. However, the growing demand for truffles, combined with the reduction of natural habitats due to deforestation and intensive agriculture, led to a decrease in nature reserves.

The first experiments:

In 1808, Joseph Talon, a French farmer, noticed that truffles often grew near specific plants, such as oaks and hazelnuts. Following this intuition, he planted oak acorns in a land where truffles were already present, starting a primitive form of cultivation.

Later, Auguste Rousseau perfected Talon's method, successfully planting trees in mycorrhizal soils. This marked the starting point for modern truffle cultivation.

The scientific development of truffle cultivation

Starting from the second half of the nineteenth century, scientific interest in truffle cultivation increased. Advances in mycology made it possible to better understand mycorrhizal symbiosis, the process by which fungi draw nourishment from the roots of host plants, returning mineral salts and water in return.

Key principles that emerged from the research:

Mycorrhization: The truffle is an ectomycorrhizal fungus, which means that it lives in symbiosis with the roots of specific plants, such as oaks, hazelnuts, hornbeams and pines. Without this symbiotic relationship, the truffle cannot develop.

Soil conditions: Truffles require well-drained, calcareous, or calcium-carbonate-rich soils, with a neutral or slightly alkaline pH.

Climate: Moderate temperatures, regular rainfall and well-defined seasonality are essential for good truffle production.

Modern truffle growing: techniques and approaches

With the twentieth century, truffle cultivation has established itself as a structured agricultural practice. The introduction of advanced technologies and the improvement of scientific knowledge have made it possible to optimize production.

1. Production of mycorrhizal plants

The first step in truffle cultivation consists in the production of mycorrhizal host plants. These are grown in specialized nurseries, where the roots are inoculated with truffle spores. The process requires:

Sterilization of the soil and seeds to avoid contamination by unwanted fungi.

The inoculation of truffle spores under controlled conditions.

A period of growth of mycorrhizal plants, during which it is verified that the symbiosis has been established correctly.

2. Soil preparation

The choice and preparation of the soil are essential. The following must be carried out:

Soil analysis to verify pH, structure and composition.

Soil improvement work, such as adding calcium carbonate if necessary.

Creation of adequate drainage conditions to avoid water stagnation.

3. Planting mycorrhizal plants

Mycorrhizal plants are planted respecting a

specific density, usually 300-500 plants per hectare, depending on the type of truffle to be cultivated. The main cultivated species are:

Prized black truffle (Tuber melanosporum): Grown mainly in France, Spain and Italy.

White truffle (Tuber magnatum): More difficult to cultivate; most of the production is still spontaneous.

Summer truffle (Tuber aestivum): Suitable for more variable climates and less calcium-rich soils.

4. Maintenance of the plantThe management of a truffle ground requires regular care to ensure optimal production:

Weed control to avoid competition with mycorrhizal plants.

Pruning of trees to ensure proper exposure to light and good aeration of the soil.

Monitoring of soil conditions and irrigation during periods of drought.

Production and harvesting

The production of truffles in a mycorrhizal truffle ground generally begins after 6-10 years from planting, depending on the species cultivated. The harvest is carried out with the help of trained dogs, which locate the ripe truffles underground thanks to their exceptional sense of smell.

Benefits of modern truffle growing

Sustainability: Truffle cultivation reduces the pressure on natural truffle reserves, preserving spontaneous truffle grounds.

Quality control: Cultivation allows us to guarantee high quality standards, with truffles that meet market demands.

Economic value: Truffle fields represent a significant source of income for farmers, especially in marginal areas where other crops are less profitable.

The challenges of truffle growing

Despite progress, truffle cultivation remains a complex practice and not without difficulties:

Long lead times: Production takes years, with a considerable initial investment and a long waiting period before the first harvests.

Environmental sensitivity: Truffles are very sensitive to climate change and pollution. Changes in climate or poor agricultural practices can compromise production.

Competition with invasive fungal species: Other fungi can interfere with truffle production, reducing the yield of the truffle ground.

Truffle growing in the future

Research continues to explore ways to improve the yield of truffle fields and adapt cultivation to new challenges, such as climate change. Technologies such as soil monitoring through sensors and the use of big data are transforming truffle cultivation into an increasingly scientific and sustainable activity.

The transition from spontaneous harvesting to structured agricultural practice represents not only a technical evolution, but also a response to the needs of an ever-expanding market, which requires high quality truffles in ever greater quantities.

Chapter 2: Types of truffles and their characteristics

Classification of truffles: white, black, summer, winter

Truffles belong to the genus **Tuber** and are hypogean mushrooms, i.e. they grow underground in symbiosis with the roots of certain plants. Their types are classified according to characteristics such as color, seasonality, aroma and commercial value. The main categories are as follows:

Prized white truffle (Tuber magnatum Pico)

Main features

Appearance: Irregularly shaped, often gnarled, with a smooth or slightly velvety surface. The color varies from pale yellow to cream, sometimes with reddish hues.

Gleba (pulp): Internally it has white and thin veins on a background that can vary from cream to light brown.

Aroma: Very intense and distinctive, with notes of garlic, aged cheese and wet earth. This scent makes it the most sought-after truffle in the world.

Size: It can vary from a few grams up to specimens weighing several ounces.

Habitat: It grows mainly in symbiosis with oaks, limes, willows and poplars. It prefers calcareous, moist but well-drained soils.

Seasonality: It is mainly harvested in autumn, from September to December.

Geographical distribution: It is widespread in Italy (especially Piedmont, Marche, Umbria and Tuscany) and in some limited areas of Eastern Europe.

Commercial value

The white truffle is considered the most valuable and expensive, thanks to its rarity and unmistakable aroma. It is mainly used raw, thinly sliced on dishes such as noodles, risottos and eggs.

Prized black truffle (Tuber melanosporum)

Main features

Appearance: Dark, black-brown outer surface with a wrinkled, warty texture.

Gleba (pulp): Internally it is dark brown or black in color, with well-defined white veins.

Aroma: Intense and refined, with notes of undergrowth, chocolate and hazelnut. It is less pungent than white truffles but equally complex.

Size: Generally smaller than the white truffle, but even here you can find specimens of significant weight.

Habitat: It grows in symbiosis with oaks, hazelnuts and hornbeams, in calcareous and well-drained soils.

Seasonality: It is harvested in winter, from November to March.

Geographical distribution: It is common in Italy, France, and Spain, with France being the largest producer.

Commercial value

The prized black truffle is widely appreciated in the kitchen, both raw and cooked. Cooking enhances its aroma, making it ideal for preparations such as sauces, meat and pasta dishes.

Summer truffle or scorzone (Tuber aestivum)

Main features

Appearance: Similar to the black truffle prized for its color and external surface, but less wrinkled and with a thicker skin.

Gleba (pulp): Light hazelnut in colour with well-marked white veins.

Aroma: More delicate than the finest truffles, with notes of hazelnut and fresh mushrooms.

Size: Generally small to medium in size.

Habitat: It grows in symbiosis with oaks, hazelnuts and hornbeams, in calcareous and clayey soils.

Seasonality: It is harvested in summer, from May to September.

Geographical distribution: Present in most of Europe, with a good diffusion in Italy.

Commercial value

The summer truffle is less expensive than the fine black and white, but it is appreciated for its versatility. It is mainly used raw or in simple preparations, such as salads and appetizers.

Winter or brumale truffle (Tuber brumale)

Main features

Appearance: Black and wrinkled outer surface, similar to the prized black truffle, but generally smaller in size.

Gleba (pulp): Dark brown with less evident white veins than the prized black truffle.

Aroma: Intense but less complex, with notes of earth, musk and undergrowth.

Size: Smaller than premium black.

Habitat: It grows in symbiosis with oaks and hazelnuts, in soils similar to those of the prized black.

Seasonality: It is harvested in the middle of winter, from December to March.

Geographical distribution: Common in Italy, France and other areas of southern Europe.

Commercial value

The winter truffle is less expensive than the fine black, but it is still used in cooking for its characteristic aroma. It is suitable both raw and cooked, and is often used in the production of truffle-based oils and preserves.

Comparison of the main types

- **Species**
- **Color**
- **Aroma**
- **Season**
- **Value**

- **Fine white**
  - Creamy yellow
  - Very intense, complex
  - Autumn
  - Highest

- **Premium Black**
  - Black-brown
  - Intense, refined
  - Winter
  - High

Species	Color	Aroma	Season	Value
Summer (scorzone)	Light black-brown	Delicate, hazelnut	Summer	Medium
Winter (brumale)	Dark Black	Intense, earthy	Winter	Medium-low

The diversity of truffles, with their unique characteristics, not only enriches the cuisine, but also represents a valuable resource for the economy of the rural areas where they are harvested and cultivated. Each variety finds its own place in the gastronomic landscape, satisfying different palates and expanding culinary possibilities.

Description of the main species of truffles

The world of truffles is dominated by a few main species, each with unique characteristics that define its economic value, use in the kitchen and environmental preferences. Among these, the most important species are the **Tuber magnatum**, the **Tuber melanosporum**, the **Tuber aestivum** and the **Tuber brumale**.

1. Tuber magnatum Pico

Known as: Prized white truffle

Morphological characteristics:

Peridium (outer surface): Pale yellow or creamy in colour, sometimes with greenish or reddish hues. The surface is smooth or slightly velvety.

Gleba (internal pulp): Variable in colour from cream to light brown, crossed by thin branched white veins that do not disappear when ripe.

Size: It can range from small in size (a few grams) to extraordinary specimens that exceed one kilogram in weight.

Symbiotic habitats and plants:

It prefers calcareous, moist but well-drained soils, often associated with mixed forests of oaks (Quercus spp.), poplars (Populus spp.), willows (Salix spp.) and lime trees (Tilia spp.).

It grows wild in hilly areas with temperate climates and regularly distributed rainfall.

Seasonality:

It is mainly found in autumn, with the peak of the harvest between September and December.

Aroma and flavor:

It is famous for its intoxicating and complex aroma, with notes of garlic, aged cheese, honey and moist earth.

The flavor is intense, persistent and capable of enriching simple dishes such as tagliatelle, risotto and eggs.

Commercial value:

It is the most valuable and expensive truffle, with prices that can exceed 5,000 euros per kilogram, depending on quality and size.

---

2. Tuber melanosporum Vittadini

Known as: Prized black truffle

Morphological characteristics:

Peridium: Dark, black-brown surface, characterized by polygonal warts and slightly wrinkled.

Gleba: Black or dark brown in color, crossed by finely branched white veins, which become more evident when the truffle is ripe.

Size: Generally smaller than the Tuber magnatum, with an average weight of 20-200 grams, but larger specimens can be found.

Symbiotic habitats and plants:

It lives in symbiosis with oaks (Quercus pubescens, Quercus ilex), hazelnuts (Corylus avellana) and hornbeams (Carpinus betulus).

It prefers well-drained, calcareous soils, with a good level of aeration and a pH between 7 and 8.

It develops in areas with Mediterranean climates and moderate rainfall.

Seasonality:

The harvest takes place mainly in winter, from November to March.

Aroma and flavor:

The aroma is less pungent than white truffle, but just as refined, with notes of undergrowth, hazelnut, chocolate and musk.

The flavor is delicate, ideal to be enhanced in cooked dishes.

Commercial value:

It is the second most valuable truffle after the Tuber magnatum, with prices that can range from 800 to 2,000 euros per kilogram, depending on the quality.

3. Tuber aestivum Vittadini

Known as: Summer truffle or scorzone

Morphological characteristics:

Peridium: Black-brown surface, characterized by larger and less wrinkled pyramidal warts than Tuber melanosporum.

Gleba: Internally it is hazelnut or light yellow in color, with less dense and thin white veins.

Size: Generally medium-small, but can reach significant sizes.

Symbiotic habitats and plants:

It grows in symbiosis with oaks, hazelnuts and pines, in more variable soils than other species, including soils less rich in calcium.

It is less demanding in terms of climatic conditions, adapting to a wide range of environments.

Seasonality:

It is harvested in summer, from May to September, with ripening taking place in the middle of summer.

Aroma and flavor:

The aroma is delicate and less intense than Tuber magnatum and Tuber melanosporum, with hints of hazelnut, fresh mushrooms and straw.

The flavor is less complex, but pleasant, making it ideal for simple preparations.

Commercial value:

It is the least expensive truffle among the main ones, with an average price ranging from 50 to 200 euros per kilogram.

---

4. Tuber brumale Vittadini

Also Known As: Winter Truffle

Morphological characteristics:

Peridium: A black, warty surface, similar to Tuber melanosporum, but with more pronounced warts.

Gleba: Internally it is dark brown or gray, crossed by white veins less evident than the fine black.

Size: Small-medium, rarely exceeding 100-200 grams.

Symbiotic habitats and plants:

It develops in symbiosis with oaks, hornbeams and hazelnuts, in calcareous and clayey soils.

It prefers areas with cold and humid climates.

Seasonality:

It is harvested in the middle of winter, from December to March.

Aroma and flavor:

The aroma is intense, with notes of musk, undergrowth and wet earth, but less refined than Tuber melanosporum.

The flavor is more earthy and bold, but less complex.

Commercial value:

It is considered less valuable than fine black and white, with a price ranging between 100 and 400 euros per kilogram.

Comparison of the main species

Species	Aroma	Aspect	Main habitat	Commercial value (€)
Tuber magnatum	Intense, complex	Creamy yellow, smooth	Oaks, poplars, willows	2.000 - 5.000+
Tuber melanosporum	Refined, persistent	Black, warty	Oaks, hazelnuts, hornbeams	800-2.000
Tuber aestivum	Delicate,	Black, les	Oaks, pines	50-200

Species	Aroma	Aspect	Main habitat	Commercial value (€)
	hazelnut	s, wrinkled	, hazelnuts	
Brumale tuber	Intense, earthy	Black, warty	Oaks, hornbeams, hazelnuts	100-400

This classification highlights the peculiarities of the main species of truffles, making them easily identifiable for both experts and enthusiasts. Each of them contributes to the extraordinary richness of the culinary and natural heritage.

Chapter 3: Truffle Biology

1. Life Cycle of the Truffle

The life cycle of the truffle is made up of several stages that involve interaction with the roots of host plants. These stages include:

Mycelium development: The truffle begins as a spore that germinates in the soil, forming a lattice of filaments called mycelium. The mycelium expands, trying to establish a symbiosis with the roots of a host plant.

Mycorrhizal symbiosis: The mycelium forms mycorrhizae, symbiotic structures that envelop the roots of the host plant. These mycorrhizae allow a bidirectional exchange of nutrients: the truffle receives sugars produced by the plant's photosynthesis, while providing the plant with water and mineral salts.

Fruiting:
After a period of development that can last

months or years, the truffle produces the fruiting body (the edible part). Fruiting takes place underground and depends on factors such as temperature, humidity and available nutrients.

Dissemination:

Animals (wild boars, rodents, etc.) attracted by the pungent smell of truffles consume the fruiting body and disperse the spores into the soil through the droppings, allowing the germination of new mycelia.

2. Symbiotic Interaction with Host Plants

The truffle is an ectomycorrhizal fungus that lives in close symbiosis with arboreal and shrubby plants. This relationship is crucial for its development and fruiting.

Main host plants:

Oaks (*Quercus*), hazels (*Corylus avellana*), hornbeams (*Carpinus betulus*), poplars (*Populus*), lime trees (*Tilia*), and other species. Each type of truffle prefers specific host plants; For example:

- *Tuber magnatum Pico* (fine white): prefers oaks and poplars.
- *Tuber melanosporum* (fine black): it prefers oaks and hazelnuts.

Benefits for the host plant: Mycorrhizae improve the absorption of water and minerals (phosphorus, nitrogen) and increase the plant's resistance to environmental and pathogenic stresses.

---

3. Ideal Soils and Microclimates

Success in truffle production depends on the quality of the soil and microclimatic conditions.

Soil characteristics:

- **Structure:** Well-drained soils, with good aeration.
- **Chemical composition:** Soils rich in calcium carbonate (pH 7-8) are ideal. The absence of water stagnation is essential.

Depth: An arable layer of at least 30-50 cm is necessary to allow the development of the mycelium and the fruiting body.

Organic matter: Moderate levels of organic matter promote the microbial activity essential for truffles.

Microclimate:

Temperature: Prized species such as the prized white truffle require hot summers and mild winters. The prized black truffle is more resistant to extreme temperatures.

Moisture: Moderate and consistent moisture in the soil is essential. Artificial irrigation may be necessary in times of drought.

Exposure: Soils exposed to the south or south-east are ideal for ensuring the necessary warmth for the black truffle, while the white prefers cooler areas.

---

4. Factors Affecting Production

The production of truffles is influenced by numerous environmental, biological and anthropogenic factors.

Natural factors:

- **Climate:** Extreme events, such as drought or frost, can disrupt the fruiting cycle.

- **Microbial biodiversity:** A soil rich in beneficial microbes promotes mycelium growth.

- **Competition:** Other fungi or weeds may compete for nutrients, reducing productivity.

Human Management:

- **Truffle growing:** Planting mycorrhizal plants in suitable soils is a common practice to ensure stable production.

- **Sustainable harvesting:** Overharvesting without respect for ripening times can compromise natural regeneration.

- **Soil maintenance:** Practices such as clearing the undergrowth and managing pH are crucial.

Pollution and urbanization: The quality of the soil and air is essential for the development of truffles. Pollution can damage mycelium and mycorrhizal symbiosis.

The biology of the truffle is a fascinating example of the interaction between mushrooms and the environment. To preserve and improve production, it is crucial to combine scientific knowledge with sustainable management of soils and natural resources.

Chapter 4: Soil Preparation

Soil preparation is a crucial stage in truffle cultivation, as the success of truffle cultivation depends largely on the suitability of the soil, the selection of host plants, and planting techniques. This chapter goes into detail about the basic steps to create an optimal environment for truffle growth.

1. Location Selection and Soil Analysis

The position and quality of the soil are decisive for the productivity of the truffle plant. Before proceeding with cultivation, it is essential to carry out a thorough analysis of the environmental and soil conditions.

1.1. Choosing the Location

Exhibition:

- For the prized black truffle (*Tuber melanosporum*): prefer soils facing south or south-east, which guarantee greater sun exposure and heat.

- For the prized white truffle (*Tuber magnatum Pico*): prefer northern or north-eastern exposures, in areas with greater humidity and natural shade.

Altitude:

- Fine black: 300-1,000 meters above sea level.
- Fine white: 100-700 meters, with humid and cool microclimates.

Climate:

Areas with mild winters and hot summers. The ideal rainfall is between 600 and 1,200 mm/year, evenly distributed.

1.2. Soil Analysis

A chemical-physical analysis of the soil is essential to assess the compatibility of the soil with the truffle.

Key parameters:

- **pH:** The truffle prefers calcareous soils with a pH between 7.5 and 8.5.

- **Active limescale:** It must be greater than 10%, with an optimal between 20% and 40%.
- **Texture:** Well-drained soils, with a balanced composition of sand, silt and clay (sandy-silty).
- **Organic matter:** It must be moderate, around 2-3%.
- **Absence of waterlogging:** It is essential that the soil is well drained to avoid root asphyxiation.

Analysis to be carried out:

- Chemical analysis (pH, organic matter, carbonates, phosphorus and potassium).
- Physical analysis (texture, water retention capacity).
- Pedological study to evaluate the stratification and depth of the soil.

---

2. pH Correction and Substrate Preparation

If the soil analysis reveals deficiencies or imbalances, action is taken to correct them before planting.

2.1. pH correction

Acidic media (pH < 7):

- Apply calcium carbonate (agricultural lime) or dolomite to increase the pH. The amount varies depending on the acidity of the soil (generally 1-3 tons per hectare).

Soils with too high a pH (> 8.5):

- Limited interventions; Generally, the soil is not suitable for the cultivation of truffles.

2.2. Substrate Preparation

Tillage:

- Plough deeply (30-40 cm) to improve the structure and promote the rooting of the plants.
- Level the ground to ensure optimal drainage.

Addition of organic matter:

- Incorporate mature compost or well-decomposed manure if the level of organic matter is too low (< 2%).

Weed control:

- Eliminate weeds and plants that could compete with mycorrhizal plants.

---

3. Choice of Mycorrhizal Plants

The choice of mycorrhizal host plants is essential, as these determine the ability of the truffle to develop and fruit.

3.1. Selection of Host Species

Prized Black Truffle:

- Downy oak (*Quercus pubescens*), cork oak (*Quercus suber*), hazel (*Corylus avellana*).

Fine White Truffle:

- Poplar (*Populus*), linden (*Tilia*), willow (*Salix*), hornbeam (*Carpinus*).

3.2. Certified Mycorrhizal Plants

Purchase mycorrhizal seedlings from certified nurseries. These plants must be guaranteed to have roots colonized by the mycelium of the desired truffle.

Verify the quality of mycorrhizae by microscopic analysis.

---

4. Implantation Techniques

Proper planting technique is essential to ensure the survival of plants and the development of symbiosis.

4.1. Planting Density and Distance

Prized Black Truffle:

- Distance between plants: 4-5 meters.
- Density: 500-1,000 plants per hectare.

Fine White Truffle:

- Longer distance, up to 6-8 meters.
- Density: 300-400 plants per hectare.

4.2. Preparation of the Planting Holes

Dimensions: 40-50 cm deep and 30-40 cm wide.

Fill the bottom with a mixture of the original soil, organic matter and limestone, if necessary.

4.3. Planting

Position the seedling so that the collar (the base of the stem) remains at ground level.

Cover with soil, compacting slightly to remove air pockets.

Water thoroughly immediately after planting.

4.4. Mulching

Apply a layer of organic mulch (straw, wood chips) or fabric to maintain soil moisture and reduce weeds.

Preparing the soil for truffle cultivation therefore requires a combination of scientific analysis, agronomic interventions and prudent choices. With careful planning and attention to detail, an optimal ecosystem can be created for the production of fine truffles.

Chapter 5: Choosing Host Plants

The choice of host plants is one of the most important aspects in truffle cultivation, as they provide essential support for the development of the mycelium and fruiting body. In this chapter, we will examine the most suitable trees, the compatibility between plant species and truffles, and mycorrhization techniques with related certifications.

---

1. Most Suitable Trees

Host plants for truffles must have specific characteristics that favor mycorrhizal symbiosis, such as an expanded root system and the ability to establish mutualistic interactions with the fungus. Here is a detailed description of the most common trees:

1.1. Downy oak (*Quercus pubescens*)

Features:

- A species of oak found in temperate and dry climates.
- Deep and well-branched roots, ideal for the development of mycelium.

Compatible truffle species:

- *Tuber melanosporum* (fine black).
- *Tuber aestivum* (scorzone).

Advantages:

- Suitable for calcareous and well-drained soils.
- Excellent resistance to drought.

1.2. Holm oak (*Quercus ilex*)

Features:

- Evergreen oak typical of Mediterranean climates.
- Resistant to heat and dry.

Compatible truffle species:

- *Tuber melanosporum* (fine black).
- *Tuber aestivum* (scorzone).

Advantages:

- It promotes the production of high-quality truffles in hot and arid areas.

1.3. Hazelnut (*Corylus avellana*)

Features:

- Shrub with superficial and developed roots, very suitable for mycorrhization.
- Fast growth and easy management.

Compatible truffle species:

- *Tuber melanosporum* (fine black).
- *Tuber aestivum* (scorzone).

Advantages:

- Ideal for intensive truffle cultivation thanks to its fast growth.
- Suitable for hilly and humid terrain.

1.4. Hornbeam (*Carpinus betulus*)

Features:

- Deciduous tree typical of temperate climates, with expanded roots.

- Resistant to a wide range of environmental conditions.

Compatible truffle species:

- *Tuber magnatum Pico* (fine white).

Advantages:

- Compatible with white truffles, which requires humid and cool environments.

---

2. Compatibility of Plants with Different Truffle Species

Each species of truffle develops best in symbiosis with certain host plants, influencing the quality and quantity of production. Here is an overview of the main combinations:

2.1. *Tuber melanosporum* (Fine Black)

Compatible plants:

- Downy oak (*Quercus pubescens*).
- Holm oak (*Quercus ilex*).
- Hazelnut (*Corylus avellana*).

Features:

- It grows well in warm climates with high sun exposure.

- It requires calcareous and well-drained soils.

2.2. *Tuber magnatum Pico* (Fine White)

Compatible plants:

- Hornbeam (*Carpinus betulus*).
- Poplar (*Populus*).
- Linden (*Tilia*).

Features:

- It prefers cool and humid environments with clayey-calcareous soils.
- It develops in shaded areas or with limited exposure.

2.3. *Tuber aestivum* (Scorzone)

Compatible plants:

- Downy oak (*Quercus pubescens*).
- Holm oak (*Quercus ilex*).
- Hazelnut (*Corylus avellana*).

Features:

- Suitable for a wide range of terrains and climates.
- Less demanding than other species.

3. Mycorrhization: Techniques and Certifications

Mycorrhization is the process by which the roots of host plants are colonized by the mycelium of the truffle. This is a fundamental step to ensure the growth and production of truffles.

3.1. Mycorrhization Techniques

Mycorrhization can be artificially carried out in the nursery to ensure that the plants are well colonized before planting. The main methods include:

Soil inoculation:
The truffle mycelium is incorporated directly into the substrate during the growth of the seedling.

Root Dipping:
The roots of the plants are immersed in a suspension of truffle spores.

Introduction of spores:
The spores of the truffle are distributed around the roots in a sterile substrate.

3.2. Certifications

To ensure the quality of mycorrhizal plants, it is essential that they are accompanied by certificates of conformity.

Microscopic analysis:
Verifies the presence and identity of mycorrhizae on the roots.

Genetic certification:
Validates the compatibility between the plant and the type of truffle desired.

Traceability:
Each plant must be accompanied by a register certifying the nursery of origin, the method of mycorrhization and the controls carried out.

The choice of host plants and their correct mycorrhization are essential for the success of truffle growing. Opting for well-compatible species, from certified nurseries, guarantees not only a high probability of fruiting, but also the sustainability of the plant in the long term. With this in mind, truffle production can be optimized for excellent quality and quantity.

Chapter 6: Management of the Truffle Ground

Truffle farm management requires an integrated approach that includes irrigation, plant care, weed control, and continuous monitoring of soil health. These aspects are essential to maintain a favorable environment for truffle production and to optimize the quality and quantity of the harvest.

1. Irrigation and Water Management

Water availability is one of the main factors for the success of a truffle farm. Water management must be calibrated to meet the needs of mycorrhizal plants and truffle mycelium, avoiding both excess and deficiency.

1.1. Water requirements of truffles

Truffles need constant moisture in the soil during critical stages of development:

- **Spring:** Stimulation of mycelium growth.

- **Summer:** Formation and development of the fruiting body.
- **Autumn:** Maturation of the truffle.

A water deficit can compromise production, while an excess can promote the proliferation of pathogens or stagnation.

1.2. Irrigation Techniques

Drip irrigation: It is the most effective method to ensure a targeted water supply, avoiding waste and stagnation.

- Place drippers near the collar of plants to keep moisture constant in the root zone.

Sprinkler irrigation: Simulates natural rainfall, but can promote weed growth.

Moisture Sensors: Install sensors in the soil to monitor the moisture level and activate irrigation only when necessary.

1.3. Frequency and quantity

It depends on the type of soil and climatic conditions.

In summer, it is advisable to irrigate once or twice a week with 15-30 mm of water.

2. Pruning and Plant Care

Pruning of host plants is essential to control growth, optimize photosynthesis, and ensure good development of mycorrhizal symbiosis.

2.1. Objectives of pruning

Improve sunlight penetration: Light promotes mycelium growth and the ideal temperature in the soil.

Reduce root competition: Limit root overgrowth to promote the relationship between mycelium and plants.

Control air growth: Too dense canopy increases humidity and the risk of fungal diseases.

2.2. Types of pruning

Formation pruning: In the early years, to create a balanced canopy structure.

Maintenance pruning:
Remove dry, damaged, or too low branches.

Root pruning (if necessary):
Interventions on the root system to stimulate mycorrhization.

2.3. Pruning period

Pruning in winter or early spring, when the plants are in vegetative rest.

---

3. Weed Control

Weeds compete with host plants for resources, limiting mycelium growth and altering soil microclimatic conditions.

3.1. Control methods

Organic mulching:

- Apply a layer of organic material (e.g., straw, dry leaves) around the plants to reduce weed growth and maintain moisture.

Artificial mulching:

- Use non-woven fabric or biodegradable plastic sheets to prevent weed germination.

Manual weeding:
- Manually remove weeds around the plants, avoiding damaging the roots.

Chemical Weeding (Limited):
- Use selective herbicides only in extreme cases and away from the roots.

3.2. Frequency

Check for weeds regularly, especially in spring and autumn, when competition is greatest.

---

4. Soil Health Monitoring

The health of the soil is essential to ensure good productivity of the truffle farm. Continuous monitoring allows you to identify any problems and intervene promptly.

4.1. Parameters to be checked

Soil pH:
- It must remain between 7.5 and 8.5. Monitor the pH once or twice a year and correct it with limescale amendments if necessary.

Soil structure:
- Check that the soil remains soft and well-drained. Avoid compaction with light machining.

Organic matter:
- Maintain a balanced level (2-3%) with the addition of compost or well-ripened manure if necessary.

Mycorrhization:
- Take root samples to check for mycorrhizal presence and viability.

4.2. Control of pathogens and pests

Fungal pathogens:
- Monitor for the presence of harmful fungi and intervene with specific treatments, if necessary.

Insects and animals:
- Protect the truffle ground from insects or burrowing animals (wild boars, rodents) with fences and traps.

4.3. Periodic reviews

Carry out chemical-physical analyses of the soil every 2-3 years to identify deficiencies or imbalances.

The management of the truffle ground is therefore a process that requires constant attention and targeted interventions. With proper water management, regular plant care, effective weed control, and accurate soil monitoring, a stable and productive ecosystem can be created, optimizing truffle yields. Continuous maintenance ensures not only quality production but also the long-term sustainability of the truffle ground.

Chapter 7: Diseases and Pests

Truffle production can be impaired by a number of diseases, pests, and adverse environmental factors. Identifying threats early and adopting prevention and control strategies is essential to ensure the health of the truffle farm. This chapter provides a detailed analysis of the main problems, prevention methods and available treatments, both biological and chemical.

1. Main Threats to Truffle Production

The main threats to truffle production can be divided into three categories: fungal pathogens, animal parasites and environmental issues.

1.1. Fungal Pathogens

Pathogenic fungi compete directly with the truffle mycelium, reducing its ability to colonize the soil and roots of host plants.

Phytophthora spp.:
- It causes root rot and can kill host plants.
- It manifests itself with yellowing of the leaves, wilting and death of the roots.

Armillaria mellea (Wood rot):
- A fungus that attacks the root system of host trees, causing rot.

Fusarium spp.:
- It can interfere with the development of the truffle mycelium.

1.2. Animal Parasites

Burrowing animals and insects pose a threat to both mature truffles and mycelium.

Insects (truffle flies, beetles):
- The larvae of some species of flies (*Suillia gigantea*, *Helomyza tuberivora*) feed directly on truffles, causing structural damage.

Nematodes:

- Microscopic pests that attack the roots of host plants and can reduce the viability of mycorrhizae.

Rodents (mice, voles):

- They dig into the ground to feed on ripe truffles.

Wild boars and badgers:

- They can destroy truffle grounds by digging to reach the truffles.

1.3. Environmental Issues

Soil compaction:

- Reduces the availability of oxygen for the mycelium.

Water changes:

- Alternating periods of drought and waterlogging can damage the truffle.

Soil contamination:

- The use of inappropriate chemicals can alter the soil ecosystem.

2. Methods of Prevention and Control

Prevention is the most effective method to limit the occurrence of diseases and pests. An integrated approach, combining good agronomic practices and specific techniques, is essential.

2.1. Disease Prevention

Land management:

- Avoid waterlogging through adequate drainage.
- Periodically aerate the soil to prevent compaction.

Soil analysis:

- Carry out regular checks to monitor the pH, structure and presence of pathogenic organisms.

Rotation and rest of the ground:

- Leave areas to rest to allow the soil to regenerate.

Use of healthy and certified plants:

- Make sure mycorrhizal plants are free from infection or contamination.

2.2. Pest Control

Physical Protection:

- Install anti-wild boar fences and underground nets to prevent damage from diggers.

Insect Monitoring:

- Use traps for flies and beetles to detect their presence.

Rodent management:

- Place mouse traps and voles in the most sensitive areas.

---

3. Biological and Chemical Treatments

Depending on the nature of the threat, biological (more environmentally friendly and sustainable) or chemical (to be used with caution) treatments can be used.

3.1. Biological Treatments

Organic treatments are particularly suitable for preserving the ecological balance of the truffle ground.

Antagonistic microorganisms:

- Using beneficial mushrooms such as *Trichoderma spp.* to fight fungal pathogens.
- Bacteria such as *Bacillus subtilis* to prevent root infections.

Bioinsecticides:

- Preparations based on *Beauveria bassiana* for the control of insect pests.

Compost and organic soil improvers:

- They improve soil health and promote mycelium development.

3.2. Chemical Treatments

Chemical treatments should be limited to emergency situations and applied carefully so as not to alter mycorrhization.

Selective fungicides:

- Copper-based products (e.g. copper oxychloride) to control fungal infections without damaging the mycelium.

Insecticides:

- Use targeted, low-impact insecticides, avoiding soil contamination.

Rodenticides:

- Use with extreme caution to avoid collateral damage to non-target wildlife.

Strategy Summary

Threat	Prevention	Treatment
Phytophthora spp.	Adequate drainage, soil control	Copper-based fungicides
Truffle flies	Traps, monitoring	Bioinsecticides (e.g. *Beauveria bassiana*)
Rodents	Fences, traps	Rodenticides (only in extreme cases)

Threat	Prevention	Treatment
Soil compaction	Light machining, reduction of the passage of machinery	No direct treatment; Improvement of soil structure through compost and soil improvers

Managing diseases and pests in a truffle farm requires a balanced approach that favors prevention over cure. The use of organic methods is preferable, while chemical treatments should be considered as a last resort. Constant monitoring, combined with sustainable agronomic practices, is crucial to maintaining a healthy and productive environment, thus ensuring the success of truffle production.

Chapter 8: Truffle Harvesting

Truffle harvesting is a crucial phase in the production cycle, which requires specific skills, appropriate tools and a deep respect for the environment. This chapter explores in detail research techniques, the role of truffle dogs, current regulations and optimal storage methods.

1. Research and Collection Techniques

1.1. Identification of ripe truffles

Visual cues:

- Cracks in the ground, typical of areas where ripe truffles are found.
- Changes in the surrounding vegetation: The mycorrhizal area often has a more bare soil (called *a pianello* or *burnt*).

Characteristic smell:

- Ripe truffles give off an intense aroma, which is perceived by the truffle dog.

1.2. Collection tools

Spade or "hoe" for truffles:

- A hand tool, often equipped with a narrow, pointed blade, designed to dig with precision without damaging the truffle.

Ventilated basket:

- Used to transport the harvested truffles, ensuring optimal ventilation.

Gloves:

- To protect your hands during excavation operations.

1.3. Excavation methods

Gentle digging:

- Once the area has been identified, the excavation must be conducted precisely so as not to damage the truffle or the roots.

Ground covering:

- It is essential to cover the hole after harvesting to preserve the mycelium and ensure future production.

---

2. Use of Truffle Dogs: Training and Care

Truffle dogs are indispensable for effective and sustainable harvesting. Thanks to their sense of smell, they are able to identify ripe truffles without damaging the surrounding soil.

2.1. Characteristics of truffle dogs

Most used breeds:

- There is no specific breed, but the most common ones include the Lagotto Romagnolo, the Bracchi and the mongrels.

Required Qualities:

- Developed sense of smell, docility, patience and the ability to work in collaboration with humans.

2.2. Training

Training Phases:

1. **Introduction to the smell of truffles:** Use real truffles or essential oils to get your dog used to their scent.
2. **Search games:** Hide truffles in controlled environments to teach your dog to spot them.
3. **Practice in the field:** Take the dog to the truffle ground to let him experience the real context.

Rewards:

- Positively reinforce correct behavior with rewards, such as food or games.

2.3. Truffle dog care

Feeding:

- A balanced, nutrient-dense diet to support the energy needed during research.

Health and well-being:

- Regular visits to the vet and protection against parasites (ticks, fleas).

Rest:
- Avoid sessions that are too long so as not to stress the animal.

---

3. Collection Policies

The collection of truffles is regulated at national and regional level, with the aim of ensuring the sustainability of production and preserving the truffle grounds.

3.1. Permits and licenses

It is necessary to obtain a **qualification card**, issued by the competent authorities, which certifies the collector's knowledge of the collection standards and techniques.

The card has limited validity and must be renewed periodically.

3.2. Rules on collection

Seasonality:
- Each species of truffle has a specific harvesting period, defined by regional laws. Off-season harvesting is strictly prohibited.

Times:
- In many regions, collection is only allowed during daylight hours to reduce the impact on the ecosystem.

Maximum quantities:
- A daily limit is often set to avoid overexploitation.

Bans:
- The use of unauthorized tools (e.g. spades that are too large) that could damage the mycelium is prohibited.

3.3. Penalties

Illegal harvesting, damaging truffle grounds, or exceeding the permitted quantities can result in significant fines and, in some cases, criminal consequences.

---

4. Truffle Storage After Harvesting

Truffles are delicate products that require specific preservation methods to preserve their aroma and freshness.

4.1. Handling after harvesting

Preliminary cleaning:

- Gently remove the soil with a soft brush, avoiding washing the truffles except immediately before consumption.

Selection:

- Separate damaged or less valuable truffles to allocate them to different uses (e.g. transformation into derivative products).

4.2. Storage methods

In the refrigerator:

- Store the truffles in an airtight container, wrapped in paper towels changed daily, for a duration of 5-10 days.

Freezing:

- For longer storage, truffles can be frozen whole or grated.
- Store in vacuum containers or bags specifically designed for food.

In oil or butter:
- Soak the truffles in olive oil or butter to preserve their aroma, but with a limited shelf life of a few weeks.

Freeze-drying:
- Advanced technique to prolong the preservation while maintaining the aroma, used especially for truffles intended for international sale.

4.3. Aroma storage

- Avoid storing truffles near foods with strong odors, as they tend to absorb them easily.

Truffle harvesting is a practice that requires respect for the environment, technical knowledge and attention to detail. The use of well-trained dogs and compliance with regulations not only protect the ecosystem of truffle fields but also ensure sustainable harvesting. Proper storage allows the organoleptic characteristics of the truffle to be kept intact, enhancing it both from a culinary and economic point of view.

Chapter 9: Economic and Commercial Aspects

Truffles are one of the most prized agricultural products, with a dynamic market characterized by high demand, high prices, and significant opportunities both locally and internationally. This chapter analyzes the economic and commercial aspects related to the production, sale and distribution of truffles.

1. Truffle Market: Supply, Demand and Prices

1.1. Market demand

- **Global Growth:**
    - The demand for truffles is steadily increasing, especially in luxury markets such as Europe, the United States, Japan and China.

Fresh vs Processed Truffle:

- Fresh truffles are highly sought after by haute cuisine restaurants and high-end consumers.
- Processed products (truffle oil, sauces, creams) expand the range of uses and market segments.

1.2. Market supply

Limited production:

- The availability of truffles is influenced by seasonality and climatic conditions, making the supply often insufficient compared to demand.

Wild vs cultivated truffles:

- Wild truffles, harvested in the wild, still represent a significant share of the market, but truffle cultivation is growing to meet the growing demand.

1.3. Prices

Determining variables:

- **Truffle species:** The prized white truffle (*Tuber magnatum Pico*) is the most expensive, with prices that can exceed €5,000/kg.

- **Quality:** The scent, texture, and integrity of the truffle affect the price.
- **Seasonality:** Limited availability during the season increases its value.
- **Geographical area:** Truffles from famous areas (e.g. Alba in Italy) can reach higher prices thanks to their reputation.

---

2. How to Start a Truffle Growing Business

Starting a truffle growing business requires careful planning, initial investments and a good knowledge of agronomic techniques.

2.1. Initial planning

Market Analysis:

- Identify potential buyers (restaurants, distributors, exporters) and assess local and international demand.

Choice of truffle species:
- Rely on climate, available land and market demand to choose between prized black truffles, summer truffles or other species.

Cost estimation:
- The initial costs include the purchase of the land, preparation, mycorrhizal plants and the necessary infrastructure.

2.2. Technical requirements

Terrain:
- Select a soil with characteristics suitable for the cultivation of the chosen truffle.

Truffle Farm:
- Use certified mycorrhizal plants to maximize the chances of success.

Monitoring and maintenance:
- The business requires constant management to optimize production.

2.3. Production time

Truffles take a few years to develop:
- **Fine black truffle:** 5-7 years.
- **Fine white truffle:** 8-10 years.

3. Certifications and Direct Sales

3.1. Certifications

Mycorrhizal plants:

- Buying certified plants is essential to ensure quality and compatibility with the chosen truffle.

Product certifications:

- To increase credibility in the market, certifications of origin or organic can be obtained.
- Some truffles are recognized by PDO (Protected Designation of Origin) marks.

3.2. Direct selling

Local markets:

- Participating in trade fairs and specialized markets offers the opportunity to reach consumers directly.

Online sales: Creating an e-commerce allows you to reach a wider clientele, both nationally and internationally.

Collaborations:
- Establish relationships with restaurants, gourmet shops and luxury distributors.

3.3. Events and auctions

Truffle auctions:
- Participating in prestigious events, such as the World Alba White Truffle Auction, can increase the visibility and value of the product.

4. Export Opportunities

Exports represent a great opportunity for truffle producers, thanks to the growing international demand.

4.1. Key markets

Europe:
- Italy and France are well-established markets for both production and consumption.

United States: American food culture is increasingly appreciating truffles, especially in the luxury restaurant industry.

Asia:
- Countries such as Japan, China, and South Korea are emerging as major consumers of truffles, thanks to the growing interest in European cuisine.

4.2. Export requirements

Health regulations:
- Check the export requirements for each country, including phytosanitary controls.

International certifications:
- Some markets require additional certifications, such as globally recognized organic standards.

Packaging:
- Use proper packaging to preserve freshness during transport.

  ○

4.3. Export strategies

Direct distribution:
- Sell to importers or specialized distributors.

Collaborations with restaurants:
- Supplying fresh truffles directly to high-end restaurants in overseas markets.

International fairs:
- Participate in events such as the *Salone del Gusto* or gastronomic fairs to get in touch with international customers.

The truffle industry offers significant opportunities for those willing to invest time, resources, and expertise. Understanding the market, carefully planning production and building a solid commercial network are the pillars of success. Product quality, supported by certifications and targeted marketing strategies, is essential to compete in an expanding market, both locally and globally.

Chapter 10: Innovations in Truffle Growing

Truffle growing is an evolving sector, where research and technology are playing a crucial role in optimizing production, improving the quality of truffles and ensuring environmental sustainability. This chapter explores new mycorrhization techniques, the use of technology to monitor truffle grounds, and innovative practices for sustainable cultivation.

1. New Mycorrhization Techniques

Mycorrhization is the process by which truffles establish a symbiotic relationship with the roots of host plants. Traditional techniques have been refined with the introduction of scientific innovations.

1.1. Selection of fungal strains

Optimized truffle strains:

- The genetic selection of truffle strains is aimed at ensuring greater vigor, adaptability and the ability to colonize the roots.
- Certified strains guarantee a higher probability of commercial production.

1.2. Improvement of substrates for mycorrhization

Nutrient substrates:

- The substrates used during mycorrhization are enriched with natural nutrients and antimicrobial agents to promote the establishment of the symbiotic relationship.

Soil sterilization:

- Sterilization techniques, such as the use of steam or organic products, eliminate pathogens and fungal competitors.

1.3. Laboratory-Assisted Mycorrhization

Environmental Condition Control:

- Mycorrhization in the laboratory allows precise control of factors such as temperature, humidity and pH, ensuring superior success compared to traditional techniques.

Biotechnological innovations:

- The use of biostimulants and specific inocula enhances the efficiency of mycorrhization.

1.4. Molecular monitoring

DNA analysis:

- Molecular technologies such as DNA barcoding make it possible to verify the presence of truffle mycelium in the roots of host plants.

Genetic traceability:

- These tools ensure that the inoculated strain matches the desired truffle species.

2. Use of Technology to Monitor Truffle Fields

Digitalization and precision technologies are revolutionizing the management of truffle grounds, allowing to optimize yields and reduce waste.

2.1. Sensors and environmental monitoring

Humidity and temperature sensors:

- Installed in the ground, they constantly monitor environmental parameters to ensure optimal growing conditions for the mycelium.

pH Sensors:

- They measure soil acidity in real time, allowing rapid action to correct any imbalances.

Nutrient Sensors:

- They analyze the presence of essential nutrients, providing useful data for fertigation.

2.2. Smart irrigation systems

Automated drip irrigation:

- Integrated systems with climate sensors regulate water release according to actual needs, reducing water waste.

Weather forecast analysis:

- Predictive systems optimize irrigation based on predicted weather conditions.

2.3. Drones and satellite imagery

Soil mapping:

- Drones equipped with multispectral sensors analyze vegetation and terrain, identifying problem areas and suggesting targeted interventions.

Plant Health Monitoring:

- Satellite imagery can detect early signs of water stress or pathogen attacks.

2.4. Truffle Ground Management Software

Apps and digital platforms:

- Dedicated tools allow growers to record data, plan interventions and monitor the efficiency of operations.

Geolocated databases:
- They offer an overview of the different areas of the truffle ground, with detailed information on productivity, soil and climatic conditions.

---

3. Sustainability and Organic Farming

Sustainability has become a priority for truffle growing, with the adoption of practices that reduce environmental impact and ensure biodiversity.

3.1. Sustainable agricultural practices

Reduction in the use of chemicals:
- The use of organic fertilizers and biostimulants is promoted to enrich the soil without damaging the ecosystem.

Crop rotation and diversification:
- Compatible secondary crops can be integrated to improve soil health.

3.2. Water management

Water conservation:

- Using natural mulches reduces water evaporation, keeping the soil moist for longer.

Rainwater recovery:

- Rainfall harvesting systems provide a sustainable water resource for irrigation.

3.3. Biodiversity conservation

Creation of ecological corridors:

- Space is left for native plants and hedges to maintain a favorable habitat for local fauna.

Promotion of useful fauna:

- Beneficial insects and other organisms contribute to natural pest control and improve soil quality.

3.4. Organic certifications

Requirements for organic certification:

- Avoid the use of pesticides and chemical fertilizers; ensure product traceability; comply with environmental regulations.

Economic advantages:
- Organic truffles have a greater commercial value and meet the growing demand for eco-sustainable products.

Innovations in truffle growing are transforming this sector, combining tradition and technology to improve production and ensure sustainability. From new mycorrhization techniques to digital monitoring of truffle grounds, every aspect of cultivation is benefiting from significant advances. The adoption of sustainable practices and the use of advanced technologies not only increase production efficiency but also respond to the growing needs of consumers in terms of quality and respect for the environment.

Chapter 11: The Truffle Kitchen

The truffle, defined as the "diamond of the kitchen", has been the undisputed protagonist of world gastronomy for centuries. This chapter explores the history of its use in cooking, traditional and modern recipes, ideal pairings with wines and other dishes, and the best techniques for preserving and transforming it.

1. Gastronomic History of the Truffle

1.1. Antiquity and the Middle Ages

Ancient origins:

- The Egyptians were among the first to consume truffles, considering them a gift from the gods. They consumed them raw or marinated in fat.

Greece and Rome:

- The Greeks considered them aphrodisiacs, while the Romans, such as Pliny the Elder, praised their organoleptic and medicinal properties. They were often paired with honey and wine.

Decline in the Middle Ages:

- Their popularity declined, as they were associated with mysteries and superstitions. However, they remained appreciated in the noble courts.

1.2. Renaissance and Modern Age

Rediscovery of the truffle:

- During the Renaissance, the truffle returned to the center of aristocratic cuisine, thanks to chefs such as Bartolomeo Scappi, chef of the popes.

Expansion in Europe:

- France and Italy became the main countries of production and consumption, with the white truffle of Alba and the black truffle of Périgord among the most famous.

1.3. Contemporary Era

Symbol of luxury:

- Today, truffles are synonymous with gourmet and high-quality cuisine, present on the menus of the best restaurants in the world.

---

2. Traditional and Modern Recipes

2.1. Traditional recipes

Tagliolini with white truffle:
- The simpler the preparation, the more the truffle can express its aroma. The tagliolini are seasoned with melted butter and a generous grating of white truffle (*Tuber magnatum*).

Eggs with truffles:
- Scrambled or fried eggs are enriched with black or white truffle flakes.

-

Truffle risotto:
- White risotto is perfect for enhancing the flavor of truffles, seasoned with butter and Parmigiano Reggiano.

2.2. Modern recipes

Meat carpaccio with truffle:
- Thin slices of raw beef are seasoned with extra virgin olive oil, parmesan flakes and black summer truffle (*Tuber aestivum*).

Fish and truffle tartare:
- Unusual combinations such as tuna or salmon tartare with truffle flakes create an innovative combination.

Creams and sauces:
- Truffle creams, combined with cheeses or flavored butters, are increasingly popular in contemporary cuisine.

---

3. Pairings with Wines and Other Dishes

3.1. Wine pairings

White truffle:
- It requires structured white wines, such as Barolo Bianco or Chardonnay, which balance its intense aroma.

Prized black truffle:

- It goes well with full-bodied and complex red wines, such as Barolo, Brunello di Montalcino or Bordeaux.

Black summer truffle:

- The delicacy of this truffle goes well with dry white wines, such as Sauvignon Blanc or Vermentino.

3.2. Pairings with other dishes

Pasta and rice:

- Perfect for enhancing the flavor of the truffle thanks to their neutrality.

Meat:

- The black truffle goes well with red meats, roasts or game.

Cheese:

- Fresh cheeses such as burrata or ricotta can be embellished with grated truffles.

Eggs and potatoes:

- Simple dishes that enhance the flavor of the white truffle.

4. Preservation and Processing of the Truffle

4.1. Storing fresh truffles

Traditional method:

- Wrap the truffle in paper towels, changing it daily, and store it in an airtight container in the refrigerator.
- Duration:
    - White truffle: 7-10 days.
    - Black truffle: up to 2 weeks.

Vacuum storage:

- Keep the truffle fresh for longer periods, preserving its aromas.

Freezing:

- The truffle can be grated and frozen in small portions, but it will lose some of its aroma.

4.2. Transformation

Creams and sauces:

- The truffle is mixed with olive oil or butter to create spreads and condiments.

Storage in oil or butter:
- Fresh truffles can be preserved in extra virgin olive oil or clarified butter to prolong its use.

Drying:
- The truffles are dried and processed into powders to flavor dishes in a practical way.

Flavouring:
- Truffle-flavored oils and salts are derived products that are increasingly in demand.

4.3. Packaging and sales

Vacuum packs:
- Ideal for selling fresh truffles over long distances.

Processed products:
- The industry offers a wide range of truffle-based products, from flavored honey to ready-made creams, to diversify the offer.

The truffle is a precious ingredient, whose gastronomic history is steeped in tradition and innovation. The recipes and combinations enhance its versatility, making it suitable for both classic and contemporary cuisine. Its preservation and processing allow its unique characteristics to be appreciated even out of season, expanding the possibilities of use and the market. Because the truffle is not just a food: it is a sensory experience.

Chapter 12: Experiences and Testimonies

The world of truffle growing is enriched by the experiences and stories of those who have chosen to devote themselves to this fascinating and complex practice. In this chapter, we collect stories from experienced truffle growers, explore the successes and difficulties of starting a truffle farm, and share practical advice for those new to the business.

---

1. Tales of Expert Truffle Growers

1.1. An art that requires patience

Many truffle growers emphasize that patience is an essential virtue in this field. **Giovanni Rossi**, a truffle grower from Tuscany with over 30 years of experience, says:

"When I planted my first mycorrhizal trees, I waited almost ten years before I saw the first fruits. Those first truffles were the confirmation that my work and dedication were paying off."

1.2. Passion and tradition

For others, such as **Maria Lancellotti**, a truffle grower from Piedmont, truffle cultivation is a family legacy:

"My grandfather collected wild truffles, but I decided to create a truffle ground to stabilize production. It's a demanding job, but every time I find a truffle I feel like I'm sharing a moment with past generations."

1.3. Climate challenges

Many truffle growers highlight how climate change is affecting production. **Franco De Santis**, Umbrian truffle grower, explains:

"In recent years I have had to install an irrigation system because the summers have become too dry. Water management is one of the main challenges, but it is imperative to keep the soil suitable for truffles."

2. Successes and Difficulties in Starting a Truffle Ground

2.1. Successes

Increasing biodiversity:

- The creation of a truffle ground often enriches the natural environment, promoting a healthy and sustainable ecosystem.

Personal satisfaction:

- Many truffle growers describe the unique thrill of harvesting the first truffle as an unforgettable moment.

Economic opportunities:

- A well-run truffle ground can become a profitable business, especially when associated with experiential tourism or direct sales.

2.2. Difficulty

Long standby time:

- One of the main difficulties is the time it takes for a truffle ground to go into production, which can vary from 5 to 10 years.

High upfront costs:
- The purchase of mycorrhizal plants, soil analysis and soil preparation are significant investments.

Climate and biological uncertainty:
- The production of truffles depends on multiple factors, some of which are difficult to control, such as climatic conditions and parasite attacks.

Competition and fraud:
- The truffle market is competitive, and truffle growers face the risk of fraud related to the sale of non-certified mycorrhizal plants or low-quality truffles.

---

3. Practical Tips for Newbies

3.1. Careful planning

Soil analysis:
- Before starting a truffle farm, invest in a detailed soil analysis to check compatibility with the desired truffle species.

Choice of location:

- Prefer areas with a suitable microclimate, good sun exposure and access to water resources.

3.2. Gradual start

Start with a small plot:

- For beginners, it is advisable to start a smaller-scale truffle farm to gain experience and reduce economic risks.

Experiment with different plants:

- Test different host plants (e.g. downy oak, holm oak and hazelnut) to identify the most suitable ones for your soil.

3.3. Continuing education

Attending courses:

- Participate in truffle growing seminars or workshops organized by experts in the field.

Collaborate with other truffle growers:

- Talking to those who have more experience can offer valuable suggestions and practical help.

3.4. Professional management

Rely on expert technicians:

- Involve agronomists specialized in the planting and management phase of the truffle farm.

Monitor the soil:

- Regularly check humidity, pH, and nutrient levels to maintain optimal conditions.

3.5. Protection and security

Fencing the truffle ground:

- Protect the area from wild animals and theft.

Know your local regulations:

- Familiarize yourself with the laws governing truffle cultivation and truffle harvesting.

The experiences and testimonies of truffle growers show that truffle growing is a complex but rewarding practice. Successes come with dedication, expertise and a systematic approach, while difficulties can be mitigated with careful planning and the adoption of good practices. For newbies, the main advice is to start with humility and curiosity, learning from the experiences of those who have already traveled this path. The journey into truffle growing, although long and challenging, offers a unique connection with nature and a product of unparalleled value.